iBRAND™

LIFEPLAN

A workbook for building your LifePlan on where you want to be…
not where you are today.

by
Pamela Sain & Olivia Sain

www.iBrandNextGen.com

LifePlan

www.iBrandNextGen.com

ISBN: 978-1543294453

Credits
Design, Art Direction, and Production   Melissa Cabana, Back Porch Creative, Frisco, TX
info@BackPorchCreative.com

Introduction

In the Words of Gary Sain

Do you realize most of us spend more time planning a vacation than we do planning our lives?

What do you want to achieve in life? How do you want your life to be replayed when you are 90? Do you have a written plan to get there? Do you hold yourself accountable?

Your **LifePlan** can be just a couple of pages on the brand I call *You*. It's a living document, which may change many times based on your life. **Yes, life comes at you fast**! Expect the unexpected!

Your **LifePlan** should address a time frame … say five years. I know it's difficult to look into the future. However, each of you should fast forward your thinking. What lifestyle do you want? Will you be living your dream or getting closer to it?

Build your **LifePlan** on where you want to be … **not where you are today**. Envision what you want to become. **Plan it and execute it!**

If it isn't in writing, it doesn't exist.

If today were the last day of your life,
*would you want to do what you are about to **do today?***
— STEVE JOBS

Purpose

What do I want from my life?
What is my life about?
What drives me?
Why do I work?

Personal _____

_____

_____

_____

_____

_____

_____

_____

_____

Business _____

_____

_____

_____

_____

_____

_____

_____

_____

If you can dream it, you can do it.
Remember that this whole thing started with a dream and **a mouse**.
– WALT DISNEY

Vision/Goals

What do I want to achieve?
What do I want to create?
What are my dreams?

Personal _____

_____

_____

_____

_____

_____

_____

_____

_____

_____

Business _____

_____

_____

_____

_____

_____

_____

_____

_____

_____

_____

If it isn't in writing, it doesn't exist.

Notes

> Integrity is doing the right thing,
> even when no one is watching.
> – C.S. LEWIS

Values

What do I hold to be true?
What is important to me?
What am I willing/not willing to do?

My Top 7 Most Important Values

1. _____

2. _____

3. _____

4. _____

5. _____

6. _____

7. _____

If it isn't in writing, it doesn't exist.

Notes

Mentors/Coaches

Who can I confide in?_____

Who do I look up to?_____

How do they inspire me?_____

_____

How will they impact my future growth?_____

_____

_____

What have I learned from them?_____

_____

_____

Who can I confide in?_____

Who do I look up to?_____

How do they inspire me?_____

_____

How will they impact my future growth?_____

_____

_____

What have I learned from them?_____

_____

_____

If it isn't in writing, it doesn't exist.

Notes

> Don't be the best at what you do, be the only one at what you **do**.
> – JERRY GARCIA

What are My Greatest Strengths?

If it isn't in writing, it doesn't exist.

Our greatest weakness lies in giving up.
The most certain way to succeed is always to try just one more time.
– THOMAS EDISON

What are My Weaknesses?

How can I improve?

_____

_____

_____

_____

_____

_____

_____

_____

_____

What are My Short Term Goals?

Education _____

_____

_____

_____

_____

Business _____

_____

_____

_____

_____

Personal _____

_____

_____

_____

_____

Other _____

_____

_____

_____

_____

If it isn't in writing, it doesn't exist.

What are My Long Term Goals?

Education _____

_____

_____

_____

_____

Business _____

_____

_____

_____

_____

Personal _____

_____

_____

_____

_____

Other _____

_____

_____

_____

_____

If it isn't in writing, it doesn't exist.

Recap of My Experience/Expertise

When was the last time I updated my resume?
What am I doing/planning to increase my educational portfolio?

If it isn't in writing, it doesn't exist.

Notes

What Do I Need to Achieve
Short Term Goals?

Education _____

_____

_____

_____

_____

Business _____

_____

_____

_____

_____

Personal Development _____

_____

_____

_____

_____

Other _____

_____

_____

_____

_____

What Do I Need to Achieve
Long Term Goals?

Education _____

_____

_____

_____

_____

Business _____

_____

_____

_____

_____

Personal Development _____

_____

_____

_____

_____

Other _____

_____

_____

_____

_____

What are My Top 5 Leadership Standards?

Standards are how you do what you do. They are your personal benchmarks or individual commitments you make to yourself. They are your code of individual performance.

(i.e., spending quality time with staff)

1. _____

2. _____

3. _____

4. _____

5. _____

What are My Top 5 Customer Service Standards?

Standards are how you do what you do. They are your personal benchmarks or individual commitments you make to yourself. They are your code of individual performance.

(i.e., resolving problems on the spot)

1. _____

2. _____

3. _____

4. _____

5. _____

What are My Top 5 Sales/Marketing Standards?

Standards are how you do what you do. They are your personal benchmarks or individual commitments you make to yourself. They are your code of individual performance.

(i.e., make one new sales contact per day)

1. _____

2. _____

3. _____

4. _____

5. _____

If it isn't in writing, it doesn't exist.

What are My Top 5 Team Standards?

Standards are how you do what you do. They are your personal benchmarks or individual commitments you make to yourself. They are your code of individual performance.

(i.e., Am I a team player?)

1. _____

2. _____

3. _____

4. _____

5. _____

What are My Top 5 Personal Standards?

Standards are how you do what you do. They are your personal benchmarks or individual commitments you make to yourself. They are your code of individual performance.

(i.e., returning phone calls within 4 hrs., returning emails within 24 hrs.)

1. _____

2. _____

3. _____

4. _____

5. _____

If it isn't in writing, it doesn't exist.

What are My Top 5 Family Standards?

Standards are how you do what you do. They are your personal benchmarks or individual commitments you make to yourself. They are your code of individual performance.

(i.e., quality time per week)

1. _____

2. _____

3. _____

4. _____

5. _____

What are My Top 5 Relationship Standards?

Standards are how you do what you do. They are your personal benchmarks or individual commitments you make to yourself. They are your code of individual performance.

(i.e., Am I trustworthy in everything I do?)

1. _____

2. _____

3. _____

4. _____

5. _____

If it isn't in writing, it doesn't exist.

Notes

The key is to set realistic customer expectations,
and then not to just meet them, but to exceed them –
preferably in unexpected and helpful ways.
– RICHARD BRANSON

Creating WOW Experiences

*Every interaction with your stakeholders affords you the opportunity to
deliver WOW experiences. The key is to under-promise and over-deliver.
List how you can create these unforgettable experiences with your stakeholders.*

Your Boss _____

_____

_____

_____

_____

_____

_____

_____

Your Customers _____

_____

_____

_____

_____

_____

_____

_____

_____

_____

If it isn't in writing, it doesn't exist.

Your Peers

Others

What is My Style?

Style is your personal trademark.

What presentation skills do I need to enhance to meet short/long term goals?

Grooming/Wardrobe _____

_____

_____

_____

_____

_____

_____

Health _____

_____

_____

_____

_____

_____

_____

_____

Speaking/Writing Skills _____

_____

_____

_____

_____

_____

_____

_____

What is My Style?

Style is how you relate to others.

What etiquette skills do I need to enhance to meet short/long term goals?

Language/Geographical/Cultural _____

_____

_____

_____

_____

_____

_____

Technology _____

_____

_____

_____

_____

_____

Rules of Engagement _____

_____

_____

_____

_____

_____

_____

What is My Style?

Style connects you to your desired audience.

Am I prepared attitudinally to meet short/long term goals?
What do I need to do?

Is my enthusiasm contagious? _____

Am I flexible/adaptable? _____

Am I an optimist? _____

Am I a "can-do" person? _____

Am I open to new learnings? _____

Do I plan for the unexpected? _____

How much time do I spend in creative thinking?

_____

When was the last time I brought a new idea to the table?

_____

Am I committed to excellence in everything I do? _____

Do I have a "me" attitude or a "we" attitude? _____

Notes

I promise to do **WHAT** I said I was going to do
WHEN I said I was going to do it and
HOW I said I was going to do it.

My Brand Promise

Boss

What is my boss' perception of me?

_____
_____
_____
_____
_____

What do I need to change/improve/add?

_____
_____
_____
_____
_____

What is my brand promise to my boss?

_____
_____
_____
_____
_____

I promise to do **WHAT** I said I was going to do
WHEN I said I was going to do it and
HOW I said I was going to do it.

My Brand Promise

Peers

What are my peers' perception of me?

_____
_____
_____
_____
_____

What do I need to change/improve/add?

_____
_____
_____
_____
_____

What is my brand promise to my peers?

_____
_____
_____
_____
_____

I promise to do **WHAT** I said I was going to do
WHEN I said I was going to do it and
HOW I said I was going to do it.

My Brand Promise

Customers

What are my customers' perception of me?

_____
_____
_____
_____
_____

What do I need to change/improve/add?

_____
_____
_____
_____
_____

What is my brand promise to my customers?

_____
_____
_____
_____
_____

I promise to do **WHAT** I said I was going to do
WHEN I said I was going to do it and
HOW I said I was going to do it.

My Brand Promise

Social Media

What are my followers' perception of me?

_____

_____

_____

_____

_____

What do I need to change/improve/add?

_____

_____

_____

_____

_____

How would my current/future employer perceive my profiles?

_____

_____

_____

_____

_____

I promise to do **WHAT** I said I was going to do
WHEN I said I was going to do it and
HOW I said I was going to do it.

My Brand Promise

Other

What are my _____ perception of me?

_____

_____

_____

_____

_____

What do I need to change/improve/add?

_____

_____

_____

_____

_____

What is my brand promise to _____?

_____

_____

_____

_____

_____

If it isn't in writing, it doesn't exist.

Notes

What is My Brand Story?

My story is being told by my stakeholders whether I like it or not.
What do I think is my current story?

Current Story: _____

_____

_____

_____

_____

_____

_____

_____

_____

_____

_____

_____

_____

_____

_____

_____

_____

_____

_____

_____

_____

What is My Brand Story?

My story is being told by my stakeholders whether I like it or not.
What do I want it to be?

Desired Story: _____

_____

_____

_____

_____

_____

_____

_____

_____

_____

_____

_____

_____

_____

_____

_____

_____

_____

_____

_____

_____

Giving Back

Do I give back to my community? _____

What motivates me to get involved? _____

_____

_____

Is there a story behind why I chose this specific charity?_____

_____

_____

What have I learned about myself by giving back?_____

_____

_____

Is my outlook on life the same/has it changed by giving back?

_____

_____

_____

_____

Made in the USA
Monee, IL
12 January 2021